IT'S TIME TO EAT KEY LIME PIE

It's Time to Eat KEY LIME PIE

Walter the Educator

Silent King Books
A WhichHead Entertainment Imprint

Copyright © 2024 by Walter the Educator

All rights reserved. No part of this book may be reproduced in any manner whatsoever without written per- mission except in the case of brief quotations embodied in critical articles and reviews.

First Printing, 2024

Disclaimer

This book is a literary work; the story is not about specific persons, locations, situations, and/or circumstances unless mentioned in a historical context. Any resemblance to real persons, locations, situations, and/or circumstances is coincidental. This book is for entertainment and informational purposes only. The author and publisher offer this information without warranties expressed or implied. No matter the grounds, neither the author nor the publisher will be accountable for any losses, injuries, or other damages caused by the reader's use of this book. The use of this book acknowledges an understanding and acceptance of this disclaimer.

It's Time to Eat KEY LIME PIE is a collectible early learning book by Walter the Educator suitable for all ages belonging to Walter the Educator's Time to Eat Book Series. Collect more books at WaltertheEducator.com

USE THE EXTRA SPACE TO TAKE NOTES AND DOCUMENT YOUR MEMORIES

KEY LIME PIE

The table is set, the pie looks so neat,

It's Time to Eat

Key
Lime
Pie

It's finally time for a tangy treat!

Key Lime Pie, so fresh and bright,

A dessert that's sure to bring delight.

Its color is soft, a pale green hue,

With whipped cream clouds and sweetness too.

The crust is golden, so crisp and fine,

Key Lime Pie is simply divine!

Take a fork and have a try,

A zingy burst makes taste buds fly!

The lime is tart, the cream is sweet,

Together they're the perfect treat.

One little bite, and oh, what fun,

The tangy flavor delights everyone.

It's like a summer breeze on a sunny day,

Key Lime Pie sweeps worries away.

It's Time to Eat

Key
Lime
Pie

We share a slice with laughter and cheer,

This pie is the treat we all hold dear.

The whipped cream swirls and lime so bright,

Make every bite a pure delight.

The crust is crumbly, the filling's smooth,

Every piece puts us in the groove.

A dance of flavors, zing and sweet,

Key Lime Pie is the best to eat!

Around the table, we smile so wide,

Enjoying this dessert side by side.

With every bite, our joy takes flight,

Key Lime Pie makes everything right.

When the plate is empty, we'll softly sigh,

"Oh, how we love our Key Lime Pie!"

It's a treat to savor, a moment to share,

It's Time to Eat

Key
Lime
Pie

Key Lime Pie shows how much we care.

So next time dessert rolls into view,

We'll know what pie to choose and chew!

Key Lime Pie is the sweetest surprise,

A tropical treat beneath bright skies.

Let's clap and cheer, then say goodbye,

To the last sweet slice of Key Lime Pie.

Until next time, we'll dream and say,

It's Time to Eat

Key
Lime
Pie

"Key Lime Pie makes the perfect day!"

ABOUT THE CREATOR

Walter the Educator is one of the pseudonyms for Walter Anderson. Formally educated in Chemistry, Business, and Education, he is an educator, an author, a diverse entrepreneur, and he is the son of a disabled war veteran. "Walter the Educator" shares his time between educating and creating. He holds interests and owns several creative projects that entertain, enlighten, enhance, and educate, hoping to inspire and motivate you. Follow, find new works, and stay up to date with Walter the Educator™ at WaltertheEducator.com

www.ingramcontent.com/pod-product-compliance
Lightning Source LLC
LaVergne TN
LVHW052013060526
838201LV00059B/4003